BETWEEN HONOR AND IDOLATRY

How to Honor, Respect and Love our Spiritual Leaders Without Idolizing them

By

Kenneth J. West Jr

Copyright © 2014 by Kenneth J. West Jr

Between Honor and Idolatry
How to Honor, Respect and Love our Spiritual Leaders Without Idolizing them
by Kenneth J. West Jr

Printed in the United States of America

ISBN 9781629521589

All rights reserved solely by the author. The author guarantees all contents are original and do not infringe upon the legal rights of any other person or work. No part of this book may be reproduced in any form without the permission of the author. The views expressed in this book are not necessarily those of the publisher.

Unless otherwise noted, Scripture quotations are from the King James Version of the Bible. References that are marked AMP or Amplified are from the Amplified Bible, Copyright © 1954, 1958, 1962, 1964, 1965, and 1987, the Lockman Foundation, Grand Rapids, Michigan. References marked NIV are from the New International Version, Copyright © 1973, 1978, 1984, and 2005, International Bible Society, Grand Rapids, Michigan.

www.xulonpress.com

DEDICATION

I dedicate this book first and foremost to my Lord Jesus Christ. I am so thankful, humbled and honored to be a part of His Kingdom; secondly, to my beautiful wife, Joni L. West, who continually encouraged and challenged me to complete this book. And last to my incredible children, Kenneth III, Rachel, Joseph and Gloria who are the joy of my heart.

TABLE OF CONTENTS

Acknowledgements...ix
Preface..xi

Chapter One: Idolatry...................................13
  Adoration of Spiritual Leaders above adoration of Christ.......15
  The Moses Syndrome..................................16

Chapter Two: Robbers of Intimacy........................21
  Lords over God's Heritage.............................23
  Ruling versus Overruling..............................24
  Jethro Principle......................................27

Chapter Three: Positives and Pitfalls of the Fatherhood Principle ..29
  Apostolistic Fathering Restored........................29
  Extreme to Balance Extreme...........................34
  Inordinate Attachments to Spiritual Fathers..............35
  The Spiritual Daddy Syndrome.........................36
  Patriarchal Perversions................................38

Chapter Four: When Ministry Becomes Your Mistress..........41
  Beauty of True Ministry...............................41
  Definition of a Mistress...............................42
  Sons verses Ministers.................................43
  Learning to Represent the Father.......................43
  God's Will Over the Needs of the People................47

Chapter Five: For Leaders Only?.........................53
  My Sheep Hear My Voice..............................53
  Jesus, the True Mediator between God and Men...........57

Chapter Six: On Titles and Garments 61
  Titles for Identification 61
  The Word Reverend. 65
  Authority Recognized by the Spirit. 68
  Imitating the Anointing 68

Chapter Seven: Overcoming Idolatry 71
  Steps Towards Deliverance 71
  Know Yourself. 74
  Healthy Understanding of God's Authority. 75
  Subjecting to True Spiritual Authority, not Control 76
  Recovering from Becoming an Idol 76
  Seeking honor from God. 80

ACKNOWLEDGEMENTS

Many thanks go out to those who read the manuscript of this book and supplied input. Special thanks to Jim Hess, Ken Gonyer, and Jeremy and Kristin Barb for taking the time to read and evaluate. Big thanks to my daughter, Rachel West, for helping me organize and put this whole book together. May God Bless you all!

PREFACE

We live in some exciting and challenging times. These are challenges we face in our personal lives and in our nation, but it has been an especially trying time for the Church of Our Lord Jesus Christ. Recently, the Church has come under attack for its views on several institutions that it stands for, some of which include marriage, the way to salvation and the deity of Jesus Christ. So if there was ever time that we as the people of God should rise up and be a light in the midst of darkness, it is now, the hour we are living in.

As Christians, we have been presented with a unique opportunity to continue to be ambassadors for Christ and spread the Good News of the Gospel so that men and women everywhere can come to know Jesus Christ as their personal Lord and Savior. In doing this, we continue to fulfill the Great Commission left to us by our Lord: to make disciples of all men (Matt. 28:19 NIV).

There are great challenges we face from within and without; however, one of the biggest hindrances that has been observed over the years is not one from the world, but one from within the very walls of the Church. I do believe very strongly in spiritual authority and respecting and honoring those leaders that are doing their best to lead and feed the flock of God, but we have to be careful that we do not develop an unhealthy adoration and attachment to any spiritual leader, which overshadows our love and passion for Jesus Christ.

God wants first place in our lives. Matthew 22:37 says, "Jesus said unto him, Thou shalt love *the Lord thy God* with all thy heart, and with all thy soul, and with all thy mind…" (KJV). We must be ever so careful not to give ANYONE the place that Jesus Christ alone should have. This book seeks to balance learning how to give honor to those who lead us, without slipping into the error of idolizing them. May God Bless You.

*"Let the Elders that rule well be counted worthy of **DOUBLE HONOUR**, especially they who labour in the Word and doctrine"* (1 Tim. 5:17–KJV).

*" And these things I have in a figure transferred to myself and to Apollos for your sakes; that ye might learn in us **NOT TO THINK OF MEN ABOVE THAT WHICH IS WRITTEN**, that no one of you be puffed up for one against another…"* (1 Cor. 4:6–KJV).

"For when one says, "I follow Paul," and another, "I follow Apollos," are you not mere men? What, after all, is Apollos? And what is Paul? Only servants, through whom you came to believe—as the Lord has assigned to each his task. I planted the seed, Apollos watered it, but God made it grow. **So neither he who plants nor he who waters is anything, but only God, who makes things grow**" (1 Cor.3: 4-7–NIV).

1
IDOLATRY

The very word immediately brings to mind many vivid images. Webster's New Collegiate Dictionary describes idolatry as "the worship of a physical object as a god." Webster also describes idolatry as "…an immoderate attachment or devotion to something."

In the Christian world, when the word idolatry is brought up, or comes to mind, we usually think of cults where its members are forced to (or sometimes willingly) bow down and worship a false god; some made of stone, others made of wood and some made of human flesh. This image is justifiable, for there are many false religions and cults who, especially in these last days, are teaching doctrines not of God, just as the Scriptures have foreseen and spoken about.

In Timothy, the Scripture says of this, "*[n]ow the Spirit speaketh expressly, that in the latter times some shall depart from the faith,* **giving heed to seducing spirits and doctrines of devils**, *speaking lies in hypocrisy, having their conscience seared with a hot iron*" (1 Tim. 4:1-2 KJV).

However, idolatry is not always represented in such a glaringly obvious manner. You do not have to bow down and worship a stone or wooden god to have an idolatrous heart. ANYTHING or ANYONE that you put before your Heavenly Father and our Lord Jesus Christ falls under the category of idolatry.

For some, it could be their husbands or wives. For others, it could be a job or certain material possessions such as money, clothes, or expensive cars. Some even worship their own selves; however, our God is a *very* jealous God and has forewarned us in the Scriptures that we shall have NO other gods before Him *"Thou shalt not make unto thee any graven image or any likeness of anything that is in the heaven above, or that is in the earth beneath, or that is in the water under the earth: Thou shalt not bow down thyself to them, nor serve them: For I the Lord thy God am a **JEALOUS** God"* (Exod.20: 4-5 KJV).

Within the heart of a man is an inherent desire to worship. The Lord Himself placed this there, that men may learn to seek after and worship Him and Him alone.

*"He has made everything beautiful in its time. He also has planted eternity in men's hearts and minds **[a divinely implanted sense of purpose working through the ages which nothing under the sun but God alone can satisfy]**, yet so that men cannot find out what God has done from the beginning to the end"* (Eccles. 3:11 AMP).

When, men begin to forsake their God and turn their backs on Him, they must (and will) attempt to replace this desire for God with something else.

"Because that, when they knew God, they glorified him not as God, neither were thankful; but became vain in their imaginations, and their foolish heart was darkened.

Professing themselves to be wise, they became fools, ***And changed the glory of the uncorruptible God into an image made like to corruptible man, and to birds, and fourfooted beasts, and creeping things"*** *(Rom. 1:21-23–KJV).*

Adoration of Spiritual Leaders above adoration of Christ

Sadly, there has arisen another form of idolatry not as easily perceived by some and not as openly obvious as a cult group bowing down to their stone god. This form of idolatry is not easily recognized by many, because it is within the true Christian Church and that is the **adoration of our leaders above our adoration of our Lord and Savior Jesus Christ**.

Some have subtly placed their affections and demands upon God's faithful servants whom God has chosen to lead, and not upon God Himself simply because they are unable to differentiate between honoring and respecting the authority of those in leadership and idolizing them. Consequently, this has put unnecessary burdens and unrealistic expectations upon those in positions of leadership. While it is true that there are and always will be certain expectations and responsibilities placed upon leaders from our Lord and from God's people, we should not expect, or put demands on them that should be placed *only* upon our Lord. When we do this we begin to cross the boundary **between honor and idolatry**.

Good leadership should always live by example; showing the people of God how to live according to the ways of God, for their lives will be watched.

In 1 Peter 5: 2-3, the Scripture says this, *"Feed the flock of God which is among you, taking the oversight thereof, not by constraint, but willingly, not for filthy lucre, but of a ready mind, neither as being lords over Gods heritage, but being ENSAMPLES"*. The Amplified Bible here where it says "ensamples" means examples or "patterns and models of Christian living". This demand will always be upon leaders, as they must lead by example.

Yet despite all of this, they still cannot be Jesus Christ to you. **Only Jesus can be Jesus to you. He and He alone is our Rock and our Foundation. He and he alone can save you.**

The Scriptures says as much in Corinthians; *"For other foundation can no man lay than that is laid, which is Jesus Christ" (1 Cor. 3: 11 KJV)*.

The Moses Syndrome

Placing unnecessary demands upon our leadership will bring us to what is termed the "Moses Syndrome".

In the Old Testament when Moses was leading the children of Israel through the desert, he was the one who went up into the holy mountain (see Exod. 19:3, 20; Exod. 24:12-18). Moses was the one who performed all the miracles (see Acts 7:35-37). Moses was the one to always hear the voice of God (see Exod. 3:1-22; 6:1-3; 10: 1).

As it was then so it is now that many Christians want a Moses to do it all for them, and consequently they will not have any responsibility cultivating their own relationship with the Lord.

Many Christians want a leader that will be a preaching machine so they will not have to bother with the responsibility of witnessing to the lost themselves; they want a miracle worker so they do not have to bother with the laying of hands on the sick, and they want a pastor to do all the praying and hearing from God so they will not have the responsibility of learning how to hear from God themselves. They have given in to the Moses Syndrome, and while not all Christians are like this (for there are many that diligently, genuinely and earnestly seek the Lord on their own and are busy about our Father's business, doing the best they can), sad to say, many are falling into the trap of the Moses Syndrome.

When this kind of expectation is put upon any one leader, it eventually leads towards the road of idolatry, because the people of God will begin to put unrealistic expectations upon that man of God.

If that leader falls into this trap, he will then start to enter into performance orientation, where he will feel obligated to come up with a word or sermon, even when God is not speaking.

"Performance orientation" is a deadly trap and detriment to many men of God, because the root stems from a desire to please the people more so than a desire to please the Lord. It leads towards a quick road of burn-out and a loss of sensitivity to the Spirit of God. Performance orientation brings about a false honor, which brings not the honor that God places upon leaders, but one that stems simply from being popular with the people; no different than any celebrity in Hollywood. It will force a man to come up with his *own good ideas* instead of *divinely inspired* ideas that come from the Lord. Consequently, the boundary between honor and idolatry will yet again be crossed.

Men of God must learn not to give in to the pressure of performance. It will only turn into an abuse of the gifts of the Spirit that God has entrusted him with. Leaders must realize that they first belong to their Heavenly Father, not just to the people of God. GOD OWNS THEM FIRST and they are to be subject to **His Will** and **His desires** ***first and foremost.***

In no way am I saying that leaders should not serve the people of God. They are called of God to do so, just as we are all called of God to serve one another in love; but, we must remember it is God who owns us, and because God owns us, He may not always have us speaking things the people want to hear.

If leaders are subject to the people, they will always speak what the people want to hear so they can remain popular with them and not offend anyone. Some of the motives behind that is because they may not want to lose the biggest tithers in the church, for in losing that, they believe, there goes their financial security.

What these leaders must realize is that **our security** is in the Lord... in the "secret place" of the Most High (see Ps. 91:1-2). It is not in the tithes and offerings from the people that many men of God depend on from week to week. A leader who cannot speak the mind of Christ, but must constantly please the people has reduced himself to a hireling and a spiritual gigolo (pronounced *jig-gel-oh*). A hireling is one who is hired for a job. His only objective is only to gain, be it money, popularity or fame. A spiritual gigolo is one who will showboat the anointing for the same gain: both have identical goals, and both will fall into the same trap.

In order to avoid falling into this trap, all leaders must periodically check their hearts to see if their motive is to please the Lord or if it has some other plans and purposes contrary to this. If their motives are wrong, they must repent and learn to walk and please God, just like the Scripture says in John, "...*[f]or I do always those things that please Him...*" (John 8:29 KJV). Leaders should learn to do everything for the glory of God.

Let all of us follow the example of our Lord and Savior Jesus Christ, who always did those things that pleased the Father's heart.

"Furthermore then we beseech you brethren, and exhort you by the Lord Jesus Christ, that as ye have received of us how ye ought to walk and please God, so ye would abound more and more" (1Thess. 4:1 KJV).

"For do I now persuade men or God? Or do I seek to please men? For if I yet pleased men, I should not be the servant of Christ" (Gal. 1:10 KJV)

2
ROBBERS OF INTIMACY

Several years ago, I was visiting a fellowship in the Washington D.C. area. A visiting minister, Bishop so-and-so, happened to be the guest speaker at that local fellowship.

Although things did not go well with the meeting, what struck me the most was a conversation I overheard in the hallway of the church. While passing through the hallway, I encountered a group of members from the fellowship I was visiting who were contending with one of the members (let's call him Layne) belonging to the fellowship of Bishop So-and-so.

I will never forget that which I heard.

Layne, tried to explain to the local members that the only one who could hear the voice of God and give direction to the people of God was Bishop So-and-so of the church. Layne's argument: any direction or instruction from the Lord had to come from the bishop and the bishop only.

The other members fiercely contended with Layne that this was not so; that any Christian who sought after God and loved Him with all their heart and mind could hear His voice for direction in their own lives.

Not so, said Layne. "Layne went on to say only Bishop So-and-so, or men who were heads of churches could hear the voice of God and only they could give direction to the people of God for the church *and* their individual lives.

I was greatly grieved in spirit in listening to this young man, for despite being confronted by the other members with **scriptural references**, *he still would not budge in his belief.* Layne was locked-in to what he believed in.

But what's wrong with this picture?

It's sadly obvious that this young man had crossed the boundary **between honor and idolatry**. What is even sadder is that the bishop of this particular visiting church believed it himself, as did the congregation he pastored.

When a people get to a point where they believe that they must receive direction *for every area* of their lives from some spiritual leader and they will not budge in their belief, they have become greatly deceived. No pastor or spiritual leader should be speaking directives into your life constantly.

Yet many believe this.

When pastors and other leaders believe that they should speak constant directives into every area of one's life, they begin to touch a realm that should *only be reserved for the Lord Jesus Christ Himself.*

Hear O People Of God!

You may manifest Christ *yourself* through the gifts of God that He has given you to the people of God in diverse ways.

You may manifest Christ as an apostle.

The Christ in you may show himself as a prophet or a teacher.

You may manifest Christ as a shepherd or pastor or as an evangelist; however, there is one aspect of Christ that no one on Earth can ever manifest himself to the people of God as: *you cannot manifest as Christ the Lord*. **Only Jesus Christ Himself can manifest as Lord to His people.** The scriptures even warns leaders of this in 1 Peter 5:1-3 where Peter says, " *The elders which are among you, I exhort, who am also an elder, and a witness of the sufferings of Christ, and also a partaker in the glory that shall be revealed; Feed the flock of God which is among you, taking the oversight thereof, not by constraint, but willingly, not for filthy lucre, but of a ready mind, NEITHER AS BEING LORDS OVER GODS HERITAGE, but being ensamples to the flock*"(KJV).

Some leaders that fall into this trap have forgotten whose heritage the people of God are. They are God's property and leaders exist only to feed and take oversight of the flock of God. They are to lead by example, not lord over them.

<u>Lords over God's Heritage</u>

Now I will make something clear.

Spiritual leaders may give directives to the people of God as a *corporate body*, but directives to individuals concerning their *individual personal lives* do not always have to come from some apostle, prophet or pastor. **Yes,** men of God may stand up and speak the direction of the Lord concerning the local and universal body of Christ, and how the Spirit of God is moving; but, when it comes to whom you should marry, where you should live, whom you should befriend and where you should work, these directives should only be reserved for the Lord Himself to speak into the lives of His people. Although many a man of God **may** speak into individual lives, be it a prophetic word or something the Lord has revealed to him concerning another person, it should confirm something that God has *already spoken to the heart of the one being spoken to*.

Even if a prophet speaks something into you concerning your life and future that you have never heard of before (and this does happen from time to time), this should not be the norm of day-to-day living and you should *wait to see if that word comes to pass over your life*. Christians should not constantly be looking to hear a word from some man of God all the time concerning direction in their individual, personal and domestic lives. This is wrong and will lead to bondage, lordship and control instead of the freedom of Christ. *It is the way of birthing many cults in this land*, where those people will blindly follow a man, deceived into believing they are following God.

Ruling versus Overruling

Leaders must learn to rule over (1 Tim 5: 17; Heb 13:7, 17-24), not to overrule. When men of God overrule, they enter into the same mistake that many made during the late 1960s and early 1970s with the birthing of what was known as the discipleship movement. During that time, God began to restore and emphasize the biblical truth concerning divine authority, seeing as the late 60s and early 70s was one of the most rebellious times in the history of America and of the world. Unfortunately, some men of God took this truth to an extreme to which it was never meant to be taken. These men taught that people should submit to their pastors and leaders in every area of their lives and learn to be a disciple.

As their teaching began to spread, it became more and more distorted, not even so much by those who started teaching it, as by others who grabbed hold of this teaching and ran with it. It got to the point where church members were blindly following their leaders in order to become disciples of the Lord. And these leaders were telling people who to marry, where to live, what type of house to buy, where to work, what kind of car to buy, etc. I knew of a married couple involved in this kind of movement, who **let** the leader of their fellowship name each and every one of their children because he believed it was his right as a spiritual leader.

Although many men of God recovered themselves from this doctrine, repenting of this error that they had made, it had a devastating effect upon the body of Christ whose seeds still exist in some circles even to this day. The aftermath of this error also brought a reproach upon a very biblical truth called *discipleship*: Ironic, considering the word *Christian* only appears a few of times in the New Testament (Acts 26:28; 1 Pet 4:16), but the words *disciple* and *disciples* appear well over two hundred times! Jesus commanded us to go into the world and make disciples, not just converts.

"Therefore go and make disciples of all nations, baptizing them in the name of the Father and of the Son and of the Holy Spirit, and teaching them to obey everything I have commanded you. And surely I am with you always, to the very end of the age" (Matt 28:19-20 NIV).

Overall, the most damaging effect of this attitude amongst these kinds of leaders is that it robs God's people of personal intimacy with Jesus Christ. They never learn how to seek God for their own lives and families, but always have to wait to hear from the "pastor." Behind it all is a selfish, impure motive on the part of that leader as he may be seeking to build his own kingdom, as opposed to the Kingdom of God. This type of attitude benefits his own personal agenda to build a big ministry for recognition to fulfill his ego or to try to impress other men of God.

Sad to say, a false mentality and attitude has developed within the Church amongst some of the leadership, and that is, the bigger your church fellowship, the greater degree of success you have. There is this competitive spirit of constant sizing and measuring to see who can build the biggest mega-church. This gives many a carnal bragging rights attitude, and often is their own mark of approval of their success. Having achieved this so-called success, they will now get the approval of others who feel the same way that they do, and have a sense of having "made it" as doors begin to open up to them as they get the acceptance of other leaders.

Jethro Principle

Now let me clarify some things.

There is nothing wrong with having a church of thousands if God has called you to have a church of thousands. If our Great God and Lord Jesus Christ is adding and multiplying your fellowship through His blessing, that is a wonderful and beautiful thing. It is not so much the amount of people in the church as it is the motive behind why these leaders of mega churches do what they do.

If the motive is out of a pure love for the people of God and a desire to help build them up, then this is the right motive to have; however, if the motive is strictly to build a big church to gain acceptance or recognition from other well-known or popular men of God, then this is not God's way. Success is not always measured in the quantity of people a leader has in his fellowship. More so, it is with the quality of the people that are produced under a leader's ministry. It is better to have a few people who are wholly dedicated to the Lord and to helping accomplish God's purposes in the Earth than a thousand people who are not dedicated to Him, or who are luke-warm.

Remember Gideon. He won a great war against the Midianites with three-hundred strong men. It started out with roughly 32,000 and dwindled down to only three-hundred who were serious about winning a battle for the Lord. And they were successful! (See Judg. 7:1-25)

Not everyone is called of God to be rulers over thousands. Some are commissioned by God to be rulers over hundreds, fifties, thirties, twenties and even tens. See how God used Moses' father-in-law, Jethro, to break down this principle to Moses, and how Moses executed it in Exodus 18:21:

"Moreover, thou shalt provide out of all the people able men, such as fear God, men of truth, hating covetousness, and place such of them to be rulers of thousands, and rulers of hundreds, rulers of fifties and rulers of tens…"

" …And Moses chose able men out of all Israel, and made them heads over the people, rulers of thousands, rulers of hundreds, rulers of fifties, and rulers of tens…" (Exod. 18:25 KJV).

Whatever amount of people God calls us to be accountable for is what we should be satisfied with. The leaders who rule well over the tens will be just as amply rewarded by the Lord for their faithfulness as the ones who are called to rule the thousands. We must get past the having-a-big-church mentality towards one of obedience and responsibility to our Heavenly Father in whatever tasks that He may give us, be it big or small. We must get beyond being man-pleasers, and become God-pleasers.

Men of God must change their motives when it comes to building God's Church, *"For other foundation can no man lay than that is laid, which is Jesus Christ. Now if any man build upon this foundation gold, silver, precious stones, wood, hay, stubble…Every man's work shall be made manifest: for the day shall declare it, because it shall be revealed by fire; and the fire shall try every man's work of what sort it is.*

If any man's work abide which he hath built thereupon, he shall receive a reward. If any man's work shall be burned, he shall suffer loss: but he himself shall be saved; yet so as by fire" (1 Cor. 3:11-15 KJV).

3
POSITIVES AND PITFALLS OF THE FATHERHOOD PRINCIPLE

Apostolistic Fathering Restored

One of the most glorious truths being restored back to the body of Christ today is the truth concerning the Fatherhood of God. The Bible has much to say concerning spiritual fathers and fathering. Paul writes in 1 Corinthians 4:15-17, *"For though you have* **ten thousand instructors in Christ, yet, have ye not many fathers:** *for in Christ Jesus, I have begotten you through the gospel. Wherefore I beseech you, be ye followers of me. For this cause have I sent unto you Timotheus, who is my beloved* **son** *and faithful in the Lord, who shall bring you into remembrance of my ways***, which be in Christ**, *as I teach everywhere in the Church..."(KJV)*.

Although some in the church would deny that there is such a move of God on the Earth today and that the Fatherhood issue being spoken of today is not scriptural, the truth is it is very scriptural and biblically sound.

Paul's relationship with Timothy is that of a spiritual father and Timothy is a son; this is not only proven by the scripture in 1 Corinthians 4:15-17, but also in the book of Philippians. When writing to the Philippians' church, Paul made this statement: *"But I trust in the Lord Jesus to send Timotheus shortly unto you, that I also may be of good comfort, when I know your state. For I have no man **likeminded** who will naturally care for your state. For all seek their own, not the things which are Christ's. But ye know the proof of him, that **as a son with the father**, he has served with me in the gospel"* (Phil. 2:20-22 KJV).

References of Paul addressing Timothy and Titus as sons of the faith are mentioned also in 1 Timothy 1:1-2 and Titus 1:4: *"Paul, an apostle of Jesus Christ by the commandment of God our Saviour, and our Lord Jesus Christ, which is our hope; **Unto Timothy, mine own son in the faith…**"* (1 Tim. 1:1-2 KJV).

*"…**To Titus, mine own son after the common faith**…"* (Tit. 1:4 KJV).

Apostolic ministry is being raised up in these latter times. Apostolic ministry is usually raised up when the world is out of order and declining into moral decay, as, sad to say, this society is today, and even sadder to say, so is the Church world; but with this, God is raising up and emphasizing apostolic fathers in the Earth, who have a heart after God, a burden for His people and a vision to see the original patterns and principles of His Word restored back to His Church.

The true apostle does not just birth churches all around the world and leave a pastor to run the show. The truly apostolic has the patterns and principles of the Word of God birthed in their hearts. Their spirits are full of the ways of God, and they have a desire to see that which is out of order restored to order. The truly apostolic has also learned to raise what they birth and not simply abandon after they birth a church.

Jesus, who is The Great Apostle and High Priest of our profession (Heb. 3:1), was sent into the world at a time when the world was in great darkness and disorder; he challenged the world and the religious systems that held the people of God in bondage, and showed them all a better way to gain access into the kingdom of God. So grieved was Jesus with the chaos of the religious and worldly system, that He openly rebuked them (Matt. 23:13-39) and left us, His Church, with a pattern of how things should be.

Paul in the books of the Corinthians also brought some clarity on some issues within the church. He brought **understanding and order in ministry**. 1 Corinthians 12: 28-31 says, *"And God hath set some in the church, first apostles, secondarily prophets, thirdly teachers, after that miracles, then gifts of healings, helps, governments, diversities of tongues. Are all apostles? Are all prophets? Are all teachers? Are all workers of miracles? Have all the gifts of healing? Do all speak with tongues? Do all interpret? But covet earnestly the best gifts: and yet shew I unto you a more excellent way"* (KJV).

In marriages: 1 Corinthians. 7. And Corinthians 11:1-15 says this concerning marriage, *"Be ye followers of me, even as I also am of Christ…but I would have you know, that the head of every man is Christ; and the head of the woman is the man; and the head of Christ is God…Nevertheless neither is the man without the woman, neither the woman without the man, in the Lord….For as the woman is of the man, even so is the man also by the woman; but all things of God…"(KJV).*

Concerning spiritual gifts*:* 1 Corinthians 12, 13 and Corinthians 14: 1-4, 6 and 39-40 says this, *"Follow after charity, and desire spiritual gifts, but rather that ye may prophesy. For he that speaketh in an unknown tongue speaketh not unto men, but unto God: for no man understandeth him; howbeit in the spirit he speaketh mysteries. But he that prophesieth speaketh unto men to edification, and exhortation, and comfort. He that speaketh in an unknown tongue edifieth himself; but he that prophesieth edifieth the church…Now, brethren, if I come unto you speaking with tongues, what shall I profit you, except I shall speak to you either by revelation, or by knowledge, or by prophesying, or by doctrine…Wherefore, brethren, covet to prophesy, and forbid not to speak with tongues. Let all things be done decently and in order."*

And concerning finances (see 1 Cor. 9: 1-19).

So understand that when God brings the apostolic emphasis, one of its primary functions is to restore order out of the chaos that has developed in the world or in the Church.

Church also understand that this work of restoration will not be completed by just men with an apostolic gift, but also by an apostolic people, who will share in God's burden of seeing society and the Church restored to order.

Having said all this, and understanding that the apostolic is brought in to restore order, why is there so much focus on fathering and the fatherhood principle today?

The answer: because there has, sadly, been a lack of fathering both in the natural and in the spiritual realm of today's society.

So much has been said about deadbeat dads and children growing up in households without a father and consequently, it has caused many a child to grow up lacking certain aspects in their lives, feeling cheated and robbed. It has also been the cause of much rebellion in the hearts of many as they never had a father's strength and impartation in their lives. And it's hard to be a father when you have never been fathered.

The same can be said of the Church.

Many men of God are so busy building up their ministry and their own personal kingdom under the pretense of building the Kingdom of God that they have neglected the people of God whom they are supposed to be serving and caring for. They are too busy getting them birthed or born-again, but not raising and building up what they birth. They have mistakenly believed that by building a bigger building that they are building up God's Kingdom. today we have many large multi-million dollar cathedrals that have been raised up, yet there is no evidence of the presence of God there and the sheep of God have been neglected by the shepherds. They have poured millions of dollars into their physical building, but not into God's building.

Haggai 1: 2-8 says of building God's building, "...*[t]hus speaketh the Lord of hosts, saying, This people say, The time is not come, the time that the Lord's house should be built. Then came the word of the Lord by Haggai the prophet, saying, Is it time for you, O ye, to dwell in your ceiled houses, and this house lie waste? Now therefore thus saith the Lord of hosts; Consider your ways. Ye have sown much, and bring in little; ye eat, but ye have not enough; ye drink, but ye are not filled with drink; ye clothe you, but there is none warm; and he that earneth wages earneth wages to put it into a bag with holes. Thus saith the Lord of hosts; Consider your ways. Go up to the mountain, and bring wood, and build the house; and I will take pleasure in it, and I will be glorified, saith the Lord."*

Unlike the building that Haggai built for the Lord, God's true building is His people, or the Church, just as it says in 1 Corinthians 3:9:

"For we are labourers together with God: ye are God's husbandry, ye are God's building" (KJV)

Sadly, millions of dollars have been poured into brick and mortar, which will eventually fade way, and not into the people of God.

Extreme to Balance Extreme

So there has been an extreme lack of fathering in the world and as is Gods way, He always **brings in an extreme to balance an extreme**. That's why we've heard so much on fathering today. And as history has proven, any time an extreme truth is brought in, you will always have those who go off the deep end with that truth and carry it into realms that God never intended it to go; typically in today's society we call them religious zealots.

Sadly, so is the case with the fatherhood principle.

The following are just some of the dangerous extremes that I have seen during my walk with God over the years concerning the "fatherhood principle."

Inordinate Attachments to Spiritual Fathers

When leaders move into the realm of apostolic fathering, if this truth, as in any other, is not brought forth in its purity with pure motives, it can birth a hybrid seed in many that could take them years to recover from if they recover at all. We must realize that even though there are men of God called to reflect the Father in the Earth, as was Paul, Jesus still warned us through the scriptures that we are to "**...[c]all no man Father on the Earth**" (Matt. 23: 9 KJV). Yet some have, through inordinate affections, placed great demands and unrealistic expectations on their spiritual\earthly fathers instead of pressing their Heavenly Father. When they want something, they seek after that man and tug at him emotionally and spiritually instead of at their God. They phone his house constantly, or stop by that man of God's household expectantly **all the time**, always looking to get a word from Heaven. This is enough to wear out any man of God, especially if he does not learn how to shut this type of behavior down before it gets out of hand.

The flip side of this is that many men of God have their ego stroked by this and like all of that attention. So they will not shut it down, but instead allow it to get out of hand. Some men of God like that feeling of empowerment, which is a great danger to any leader who has problems handling authority. As Jesus describes in the scriptures, *"But all their works, they do for to be seen of men: They make broad their phylacteries, and enlarge the borders of their garments, and love the uppermost rooms at the feasts and the chief seats in the synagogues, and greetings in the markets and to be called of men* **'Rabbi, Rabbi'**.*"* (Matt. 23:5-7 KJV). Just like the Pharisees of old, who loved to be called 'Rabbi, Rabbi', so do many today love to be called by men **'Pastor, Pastor'**. They love the title they bear and the adulation and praise of the people whom they are supposed to be serving in humility.

Still with others, they may mistake all that inordinate attention as a sign that God has approved them, and while it is true that the anointing and the approval of God does draw people, leaders should learn to prioritize. This does not mean that men of God should stop showing hospitality as we are commanded by the scriptures to be hospitable (Tit. 1:8). It simply means that they should learn when it is the right time; but more so to learn if that person has an idolatrous heart, and is placing his demands wrongly upon them. If this is the case, it should be dealt with immediately.

I have seen people come by a man of Gods household suddenly, without any consideration for him, when that man of God was tired and worn out from ministering all day or week, and may have wanted some quiet time with his family, close friends, or just to rest and spend time alone or with the Lord, and they have pressed him nonstop for hours until they finally force that man to prophesy to them or give them a word. Usually, that word would not come out in purity because of the method in which it was released.

The Spiritual Daddy Syndrome

As the body of Christ begins to come into light and revelation concerning the Fatherhood of God and the place of spiritual fathers, another danger arises: the "spiritual daddy syndrome", where the people of God are calling their leaders daddy or father. Again I quote the scripture which says, **"...And call no man your Father on the**

Earth, for one is your Father which is in Heaven." (Matt 23:9 KJV). There are those that believe that they must call these leaders daddy and have heard some people *actually calling their spiritual leaders daddy*!

The scriptures make it very clear that there is only ONE "Daddy" and that is your Father in Heaven. GOD IS YOUR FATHER, and HE and HE ALONE is deserving of the title. So we ought not be constantly calling men by Father or daddy for when we enter into this realm, this is a breeding ground for idolatry and cultism.

While it may be true that these leaders may have a genuine apostolic call upon their lives as a spiritual father, this does not mean that the people of God have to go around addressing them as daddy or my daddy.

However, some leaders, in trying to justify this title, use the statement that Elisha said when Elijah was taken away in a whirlwind.

"And it came to pass, as they still went on and talked, that, behold, there appeared a chariot of fire, and horses of fire, and parted them both asunder. And Elijah went up by a whirlwind into Heaven. And Elisha saw it and cried ***'My father, my father,*** *the chariot of Israel and the horseman thereof'. And he saw him no more: and he took hold of his own clothes and rent them in two pieces"* (2 Kings 2:11-12–KJV).

Yes, Elijah was a spiritual father to Elisha, training him for nearly 20 years in the ways of God; however, there are no other scriptures where Elisha called Elijah this **all the time**.. Neither is there any scripture saying that Elisha went around calling Elijah his daddy. In the heat of the moment, when Elijah was taken away from him, Elisha shouted out that which Elijah had been to him for years....a spiritual father. *Nowhere else in scripture is Elisha heard saying this.*

Patriarchal Perversions

Even as spiritual fathers and sons relationship can become distorted, so can a natural father and son relationship follow the same pattern. There are those that believe that the fathers in the natural have the right to exercise their authority over their children for all their lives because they believe they are the spiritual patriarchs of the family. Now parental authority should be exercised over your children when they are small and obedience should be taught when they are young and growing up, as says the scripture, *"Children, **obey your parents** in all things, for this is well pleasing unto the Lord"* (Col.3: 20 KJV). However, if a parent or father still tries to exercise that kind of authority over his children when they are adults, married with children of their own, then it becomes a major problem! Yet I have seen this type of patriarchal perversion by some who have twisted Genesis 18:17-19 which says this of Abraham: *"And the Lord said, shall I hide from Abraham that thing which I do, seeing that Abraham shall surly become a great and mighty nation, and all the nations of the Earth shall be blessed in him? For I know him, that he will **command his children and his household after him** and they shall keep the way of the Lord, to do justice and judgment, that the Lord may bring upon Abraham that which he has spoken of him"* (KJV).

While the principle of this scripture is true, and men must take authority of their households and rule well (1 Tim 1:4-5) as well as having their children in subjection to them, this changes when that child grows up and marries, getting a household of his own. He then is supposed do as the scriptures say, *"For this cause shall a man **leave his father and mother and cleave to his wife**. And the twain (two) shall become one flesh..."* (Mark 10:7-8). There is a change in the domestic order as that man should come from under his father's rule and establish his own; however, this is not always the case.

I have seen some that have never come from under their natural fathers rule and that father constantly crosses the boundaries of his son's domestic life because of a distorted view of fathering. These fathers constantly tell them what to do, where to live, what Gods plans are for them, etc. They are constantly prophesying so-called direction from the Lord for their families and telling them how to raise their children. They never quite let go and let that little boy grow up and become a man EVEN AFTER HE'S MARRIED WITH CHILDREN. They still exercise an inordinate and unnatural amount of control over them, trying to fulfill a dual role as both natural and spiritual father.

This is a two-fold problem as the father has to learn to let go and that son needs to grow up and stop letting that father cross the lines concerning his marriage and his own household.

In no way am I saying that natural sons and their fathers should not be close. **Fathers and their sons should develop a close friendship long after they are grown up and married with children** and there is nothing more beautiful than when a young man seeks the godly advice and counsel of his father. Also, this is not to say that a father cannot advise his son on certain things he may see right or wrong in an adult- to- adult conversation. I am talking about when a man exercises a crazy kind of control over his children's family; and the children blindly follow without question!

It gets bad when that son will only move his family at the word of the Lord that comes from his daddy's mouth, and will blindly follow without question **or any reference to the Holy Scriptures.** This is definitely crossing the boundary line between honoring your parents and being in idolatry to them.

As the truth of the Fatherhood of God grows in the Earth, we must watch ourselves at all times that we don't bring a reproach upon it. We must do all that we can do to stay within scriptural grounds on this matter.

4
WHEN MINISTRY BECOMES YOUR MISTRESS

Beauty of True Ministry

One of the most beautiful and enjoyable things to men of God is the privilege to be able to minister their five-fold gift to build up of the body of Christ. Whether the gift is that of an apostle, prophet, evangelist, pastor or teacher, a ministry is entrusted to us from our Heavenly Father as it was with Paul," *And I thank Christ Jesus our Lord, who hath enabled me, for that He counted me faithful,* **putting me into the ministry**"(1 Tim 1:12 KJV). He also said in Acts 20:24," *[b]ut none of these things move me, neither count I my life dear unto myself, so that I might finish my course with joy and the* **ministry***, which I have received of the Lord, to testify the gospel of the grace of God*" (KJV).

There are other references in Scripture concerning ministry (Eph. 4:12, 2 Cor. 4:1, 5:18, 2 Tim. 4:5, and Acts 1:17, 25, 6:4, 12:25).

Ministry can become addictive, especially when you see bondages broken over people's lives and watch them set free.

*"I beseech you, brethren, (ye know the house of Stephanas, that it is the firstfruits of Achaia, and that they have **addicted themselves to the ministry of the saints,)**"* (1 Cor.16:15 KJV); however, there is another side of ministry that is not healthy for any leader and that is when that ministry becomes a man's mistress.

Definition of a Mistress

Webster's Collegiate Dictionary has several meanings for the word mistress, but the one most familiar is described as this: **A woman other than his wife with which a married man has a continuing sexual relationship.**

While a man of God may not be involved in an adulterous relationship with a woman other than his wife *per se*, he may be involved in an adulterous relationship with his ministry.

But how can this be?

Many a divorce has come about because of the constant ministering of that leader.

However, don't misunderstand what I am saying here. Ministry *is* beautiful when placed within its proper priority; however, ministry should never take the place of God or family in our lives. Yet for many it does simply because that man of God's identity is in his ministry rather than in the fact that he is a son of God.

Some identify so strongly with their ministry and what they are called of God to do that they lose sight of who they really are, and this is because there is a grave misunderstanding amongst some concerning their sonship. We must understand that any ministry not birthed out of sonship is not true ministry in its purity.

Sons verses Ministers

When speaking of sonship, we must understand the difference between sons and ministers. A son represents; a minister just ministers his gift. In other words, the leader who has had his life and character dealt with by the Spirit of God, the Word of God and through spiritual mentoring and fathering will learn to mimic what Jesus did in His relationship to His Heavenly Father, and that is to properly represent the Father on the Earth.

Learning to Represent the Father

Webster's Collegiate Dictionary describes the word represent as **"...to serve as a counterpart or image of; to take the place of some in respect; to act in the place of; to serve as a specimen, example or instance of."** To get an even clearer understanding of this, let's look at the life and ministry of Jesus Christ. In John 5:30, Jesus makes a statement revealing the way of life that He lived that should be embraced by every man and woman of God. And it is this: *"I can of mine own self do nothing; as I hear I judge: and my judgment is just, because I seek not mine own will, but the will of the Father which hath sent me"* (KJV). The Amplified Bible expounds on this bringing a greater clarity to what was spoken: *"I am able to do nothing from Myself (independently, of My own accord; but only as I am taught* *by God and as I get His orders). Even as I hear I judge (I decide as I am bidden to decide. As the voice comes to Me, so I give a decision), and My judgment is right (just, righteous), because I do not seek or consult My own will (I have no desire to do what is pleasing to Myself, My own aim, My own purpose), but only the will and the pleasure of the Father who sent me".*

Jesus perfectly represented the Father by doing only what the Father instructed Him to do. Nothing less. Nothing more. He did not confer with His own will or desires, but only the will and desire of the One who sent Him and He carried out His orders.

When a man truly learns to represent, he will not be ministering his gift all the time. He will learn to flow in *whatever state the Spirit of God has him in at that time or at that particular season.*

If it's ministering, he will minister. If it's rest, he will rest. If it's fellowshipping with the brethren, he will fellowship. If it's to spend time with his wife and children, then he will do so. Whatever God wants him to do, that is what he will do if he is a *true son.*

Yet there are many who believe they have to be ministering ALL THE TIME. They've never learned how to just shut down and be a husband to their wives and a father to their children.

As I stated earlier, so many leaders have had (or still have) bad marriages and have gone through divorce simply because they have spent more time ministering their gift then they do ministering unto God or their families. They have a warped perception, mistaking their constant ministering for obedience to God.

The Bible says in Proverbs 11.1, "*A false balance is an* **abomination to the Lord**, *but* **a just weight is His delight**" (KJV). Many leaders have a "false balance" between ministry and family life. How often have we heard from men of God who say after years and years of ministry how they regret that they did not spend more time with their families?

How often have we seen a spiritual leader go through a terrible divorce after so many years of marriage because he spent more time with his mistress called ministry then with his own wife?

We must put ministry in its proper place. It should never take the place of God and should never take the place of one's family. There comes a time when leaders have to lay down the anointing of a fivefold gift and pick up the anointing of a husband and a father.

Wives do not need a prophet or evangelist all the time. They need a husband. Children do not always need an apostle or pastor. They need a father. This is where some men get mixed up as they never learn how to change garments. They come home out of an itinerary or a revival and never shut off their gifts, and while it is true that leaders must be about our Heavenly Fathers business in the Earth, God's will is never to have a man so caught up in ministry that he neglects his family.

Now there **are times when God may try a man's heart to** see if he loves his family more then he loves Him (see Matt 10:38; Luke 14:26).

The call to discipleship is never easy and there are seasons when God may deal with a leader's life in preparation for a task He is calling him to do, or a specific ministry that may require him to separate himself even from his own family. But this should only be for a season, **a period of time** until the desired results are accomplished. THIS IS NOT A CONSTANT LIFESTYLE.

When it becomes a constant lifestyle, men of God begin to lose their interaction with their families and they grow distant. After years and years of this, the distance will take its toll on the relationship in one form or another. That's when the bomb hits them: after twenty plus years of marriage, a divorce or an adulterous affair shakes them.

Men of God must learn to minister when it is time to minister, yet rest when it is time to rest. There are times when God may call you to take a break. They must learn to pause, or take a time out for spiritual, emotional and physical refreshing.

You cannot always feel like the whole work of God or the church depends on you alone. Yet, this is the attitude that many have: that their ministry or the fellowship they are involved in is going to fall apart without them. This is not to knock the importance that each member contributes to the Body of Christ, because the contribution of each member of the body *is vital, including that of the leader*. But when one member believes he or she is the glue that holds the entire work together, this is the spirit of idolatry on that individual member. They have an exalted opinion of themselves (and others most likely only fan the flames of this opinion) and believe that they are more than what they really are.

Jesus is the glue that holds all things together. He is The Foundation of any work (1 Cor. 3:11-12), whether local, regional, national or international.

He and He alone holds it all altogether!

No individual leader can do that.

And when they try to, they then try to take the place of Jesus Christ Himself, which is something no man or woman *should ever attempt to do*. This is very dangerous ground to enter into. This is the realm where, if not dealt with, Satan can sow seeds of deception and bring in a cult mentality.

Many a move of God started out sincerely until an individual leader tried to take the place of Jesus Christ. The focus no longer became on Jesus Christ and His body of believers, but on the spiritual prowess of the individual leader. Over time, everything began to revolve around that individual leader.

When the people of God gathered in that particular fellowship, they placed all their demands upon that leader, looking to him for their answers instead of looking to their Heavenly Father. This is where lordship and control are birthed, like it did in the Discipleship movement of the 1970s, (as mentioned earlier) where the people would not do anything on their own unless the pastor told them to.

Spiritual leaders must get beyond trying to do-it-all and be-it-all. No one leader, individual, church or movement has a special corner or edge on God. No one leader is the epitome of all leaders. Some believe they are and the people that surround them believe this as well. It's a sad state that can go on for many, many years, or decades, without being challenged.

God's Will Over the Needs of the People

Above all things, men of God must learn how to rest. They're preaching six or seven times a week, counseling all the time, holding four or five bible studies a week, then flying down to other fellowships that need their help on the weekends. There are many who do not know how to just shut down or just outright say no. Learning how to say no is hard for the leader who is led by his gift and not by the Lord. They try to be a do-all to everyone, but this is impossible and a quick way to burn- out.

So how do men of God overcome this?

When they learn how to be subject to the **WILL OF GOD** and not the **NEEDS OF THE PEOPLE.**

This may sound harsh, and many may struggle with this, but **no earthly leader will be able to meet** *every single need of the every single person* **that he sees and encounters.** He may *think* that he can, but *he cannot.*

We must be subject to the will of our heavenly Father, as Jesus was; *"Jesus saith unto them My meat is to do the will of Him who sent me and to finish His work"* (John 4:35 KJV).

I'm sure Jesus, had He been led by his powerful gifts and anointing of the Spirit, could have healed everyone in the pool of Bethesda as stated in John 5:1-9. The Bible says there were a great many of impotent folks: blind, cripple, sick, mute and withered, that waited for an angel to come down and trouble the waters, and whoever happened to be fortunate enough to be there when this happened was made whole and healed of whatever disease, or ailment they had. Yet, Jesus healed only one man from that multitude.

Why?

Because *Jesus was not out to prove how gifted He was*. He was not out there to *showboat the Holy Spirit and try to prove something to man*. **But He was out to show people how to be subject to the will of God.** *NOT THE NEEDS OF THE PEOPLE!* Though He was oft moved with compassion for the people (See Matt 9:36; 14:4; 20:34; Mark 6:34), His **compassion never superseded the will of His Father**. It always coincided with it.

Looking at the life of Paul, there was a time when Paul and his companions attempted to go into Asia and Bithynia to preach the gospel, but was forbidden of the Holy Spirit to do so:

"Now when they had gone throughout Phrygia and the region of Galatia, and were forbidden of the Holy Ghost to preach the word in Asia…

After they were come to Mysia, they assayed to go into Bithynia: but the Spirit suffered them not" (Acts 16:6-7 KJV).

As the Scripture says, instead, the Lord had them go to Macedonia. No doubt, Paul's intentions were good, and there was probably a great need for the Word to be heard in those places. Yet, The Holy Spirit would not allow it at that time. Why? Paul was subject to obeying God's Will and following the leading of the Spirit of God. He was not influenced by a great need in those regions.

Leaders need to realize that they cannot do it all. We must have the heart of Paul and be led by the Spirit, not just the needs of the people. This may sound like beating a dead horse, but we've got to let the Spirit of God lead us to those needs that He wants us to meet lest we run ourselves aground and end up dry and burned-out.

Many men of God seem to feel that because they have the Spirit of God in them, that they can do any and all things. This is true to a certain degree (Phil 4:16), as the Word does say we can do all things through Christ; **but God will not give you grace to do what He has not called you to do.** No one man is a do-it-all, yet this concept has led many a man of God down the road into realms and anointing's that were not given to them by God, and it only ended in disaster and failure, because the Lord had not called them to do it.

Another good way for a leader to guard themselves from burnout or taking on more than what God has allotted them is to surround themselves with people who love them enough to confront them when they recognize that they are about to wear out and run out of steam. These should be those who have a genuine care for that leader and are joined to him by relationship.

As the Word says, there is safety within a multitude of counsel.

Proverbs 11:14 says, **"Where no counsel is, the people fall: but in the multitude of counsellors there is safety"** (KJV).

Those who develop a Godly relationship with that leader through friendship and interaction can lovingly confront him with true concern when they see that leader on the verge of being worn-out and encourage them to take some time off from their busy schedule for a season to get refreshed spiritually and emotionally and to reconnect with their wives and families.

Some leaders go on what is known as a sabbatical, which suggests a break or a literal cease from the normal routine of one's life. Some sabbaticals are planned by the leadership of their church affiliation or as they sense the Spirit of God leading them to do so.

O men of God...learn not to misplace your priorities. **Learn to put God first, family second and Ministry third, and not mingle the order.** In the end, it will preserve you, your marriage and what you are doing in His work.

5
FOR LEADERS ONLY?

<u>My Sheep Hear My Voice</u>

Concerning the concept that only spiritual leaders of the church: Pastors, bishops, Elders and various five-fold ministers that hold an office are the only ones who are able to hear the voice of God to bring direction to individual lives or to the Body of Christ; this needs to be examined in the light of the Scriptures. We need to ask ourselves *what the Scripture says about this concept.* A look into the life of a humble disciple of the Lord named Ananias will, however, refute that concept.

Before Paul became the apostle that he was, he was known as Saul of Tarsus. As a Pharisee of the highest order, he persecuted the Church relentlessly at that time (see Acts 8:1; 9:1).

But something happened to him on the road to Damascus.

He had an incredible encounter with the very One whom he was against…**Jesus Christ!** (Acts 9:3-9). This encounter left him temporarily blind (Acts 9:9). Now this is what happened afterwards:

"And there was a certain disciple at Damascus, named Ananias; **and to him said the Lord in a vision** *'Ananias'. And he said, behold, I am here, Lord.* **And the Lord said unto him** *' Arise and go into the street which is called Straight, and enquire in the house of Judas for one called Saul of Tarsus: for, behold, he prayeth, and hath seen in a vision a man named Ananias coming in, and putting his hands on him that he might receive his sight'. Then Ananias answered, Lord, I have heard by many of this man, how much evil he hath done to thy saints in Jerusalem: And here he hath authority from the chief priests to bind all that call on thy name.* **But the Lord said unto him** *' Go thy way: for he is a chosen vessel before me, to bear my name before the Gentiles, and kings, and the children of Israel: For I will shew him how great things he must suffer for my names sake'. And Ananias went his way, and entering into the house; and putting his hands on him said, brother Saul, The Lord, even Jesus, that appeared unto thee in the way thou camest, hath sent me, that thou mightest receive thy sight and be filled with the Holy Ghost. And immediately there fell from his eyes as it had been scales: and he received sight forthwith, and arose, and was baptized"*(Acts 9:10-17 KJV).

This humble disciple's obedience to the voice of the Lord was a key part in the beginning of Paul's great ministry in the earth, *but notice*; God spoke *directly to Ananias*, a disciple and gave him instructions concerning Paul. He did not speak to any of the big apostles of the day. Qualifications to hear the voice of God does not mean you have to be a five-fold minister or have the title of a Pastor, Prophet or Evangelist. **Qualifications only mean that you become a disciple of Jesus Christ** and you do not have to be five-fold to become a disciple. (reminder, five-fold ministries are the offices of spiritual leadership: Pastors, elders, etc.)

Jesus said, **"MY SHEEP HEAR MY VOICE, AND I KNOW THEM AND THEY FOLLOW ME…"** (John 10:27 KJV). He did not say "My five-fold ministers" or "My pastors and spiritual leaders" **only**. He said, **"My sheep hear my voice."**

If it is the case that all that is required to hear the voice of God is to become a disciple, how is it that some say only the senior pastor or the bishop of the church has an exclusive right to hearing the voice of God, especially concerning individual lives?

Why do countless believers cling to this fact that they cannot hear the voice of God for their own lives, but that it is reserved strictly for the spiritual leaders of the Church?

One reason is because, once again, the boundary line between honor and idolatry has been crossed. It gets that way through selfishness and deception on the part of those leaders that do so and an idolatrous heart on the part of those that believe them.

Many of the people of God that have been taught this also do not want the trouble and burden of having to seek God and hear His voice on their own. As stated in an earlier chapter, they have the Moses Syndrome. They want a Moses; leaders that will do everything and anything for them, while they accept no responsibility of their own.

Their mindset says "Let the pastor do it all...let him bring forth the Word; let him do all the evangelizing; let him do all the praying; let him do all the prophesying", and once again, an unnecessary weight is placed upon that man of God.

On the other hand, there are those leaders that love that kind of control. This is not the spiritual authority given to men of God to rule the House of God righteously according to the Scriptures, but an unrighteous controlling spirit whose base motive is either selfish gain or all out deception.

Some men of God have never been fathered nor has their soul been dealt with in this area of authority. As a result of this, they do not know how to use the authority given to them by God in righteousness way. Instead, they are like those who Jesus described concerning the spiritual leadership of His day. Matthew: 23:6-8 says, "...**And they take pleasure in and [thus] love the place of honor at feasts and the best seats in the synagogues. And to be greeted in the marketplaces and to have people call them 'rabbi'**..." (AMP). They love that title and the pride of being called the senior pastor, and the recognition that accompanies it. They love when greeted in the stores for people to come up to them and say oh...Pastor! Pastor! They love the affinity and association with their position and the feeling of power that goes with it more then they love the people of God. They are hung up on themselves and love the thrill of being in control. This is not the heart of a truly, sincere man of God, but a child who never grew up in spirit and was given authority prematurely. True to the Scriptures that says,

"**Woe to you, Oh land, when your king is a child** or a servant and when your officials feast in the morning!" (Eccles 10:16, AMP).

Jesus, the True Mediator between God and Men

While it is true that spiritual leaders are called of God to rule and take the oversight in the Church of God, instructions on how spiritual leaders are to rule is given in 1 Peter 5:2-3: "…[f]eed the flock of God which is among you, taking the **oversight** thereof, **not by constraint**, but willingly, not for filthy lucre, but of a ready mind, **neither as being lords over Gods heritage**, but being ensamples to the flock…." (KJV)

The word oversight is the Greek work *episkopeo*, which means to "oversee by implication"; to "be aware", but not by constraint or as a lord!

A Leader's primary objective is to point the people of God to their Lord and Master Jesus Christ. Good leadership always does this and has this focus in mind. Whenever a leader stands up and declares that you have to go through him in order to get direction from the Lord or to hear His voice, know of a surety that that leader is in gross deception and is being influenced by a spirit of error. In this case, you should *run*.

No man of God on Earth is a mediator between God and men. There is only One who is the mediator between God and men and that is Christ Jesus, our only Lord and Savior. Just as the Scripture says, *"For there is one God, and one mediator between God and men, the man Christ Jesus, who gave Himself a ransom for all, to be testified in due time" (1 Tim. 2.5)*.

Since when did any earthly leader give His life a ransom for the sins of mankind? No man on earth can ever conceive of claiming that right, although men can stand in the gap concerning a people (Ezek 22:30) through prayer and intercession, we must not confuse standing in the gap with being a mediator between God and men as Jesus was. To do so would be gross error.

One could also look at the life of Stephen. There is no scripture that says that he was an apostle, prophet or evangelist, and yet, before his martyrdom, he had some of the most incredible spiritual encounters.

God used him to perform great miracles (Acts 6:8), was full of faith and the Holy Ghost (Acts 6:5) was filled with divine wisdom (Acts 6:10) preached to and rebuked the religious order of their day with power (Acts 7:51-54) carried the glory of God on his countenance (Acts 6:15) and had visions of Jesus (Acts 7:56).

And all this by a man who was a church deacon! (Acts 6:1-6)

Leaders need to dispel this idea that they are the sole source for hearing the voice of God. This is an outright lie with no Biblical basis whatsoever.

As leaders, we must teach the people of God the truth. Let us not fall into the same trap as spoken of in Romans:

"Well then, you who teach others, do you not teach yourself? ....You who abhor and loathe idols, do you rob temples [**do you appropriate to your own use what is consecrated to God, thus robbing the sanctuary and doing sacrilege**]?" (Rom 2:21a-22b, AMP).

When a leader says he is the only one that can hear the voice of God, he is setting himself up as a King. We may be kings and priests unto the Lord (Rev1:5-6), but there is only one King of kings and that is **Jesus Christ**.

No man can take that honor unto himself.

When you set yourself up as the King, you do exactly as the scripture states. **YOU APPROPRIATE TO YOUR OWN USE WHAT IS STRICTLY SUPPOSED TO BE CONSECRATED TO GOD, AND THIS WILL ROB GODS TEMPLE (1 COR. 3:16-17), HIS PEOPLE OF THE RELATIONSHIP AND REALITY OF HIMSELF THAT HE SO DESIRES TO GIVE TO HIS PEOPLE.**

This is a form of sacrilege toward God, which means "theft or violation of something consecrated to God". They've caused the people of God to be robbed of true fellowship with their Creator and have knowingly or unknowingly set themselves up as the Master.

This is not a good place to be. Let us pray that anyone involved in spiritual leadership will never fall into this trap.

6
ON TITLES AND GARMENTS

Titles for Identification

I would like to touch upon an area that needs to be addressed, though it is a sensitive issue for some within the Church, and that is the area of titles given to men.

In the past couple of decades, there has been an increase in leaders who are adopting certain titles in front of their names, such as Doctor or Reverend. Many started out just being called brother, but as the years progressed and they grew in their ministries, they are now known as doctor, bishop or the Reverend-Doctor. Many seem bent on identification through a title in their local works and it is the law in many local fellowships that everyone who is a part of that work must call those in leadership by their title.

Joe Smith should not be addressed as Joe Smith. He must be addressed as Evangelist Joe Smith, or Apostle Joe Smith. Tom Jones has to be addressed as Prophet Tom Jones or better yet, the Reverend-Doctor Tom Jones.

This is supposed to bring a distinction between clergy and laity, or in other words, the shepherds (spiritual leaders) and the people of God (sheep),

Why do some men of God insist on having a title precede their name for identification when there is really no scriptural basis for doing so? Some of it is ignorance, as we have been trained for decades to believe that if a man is a preacher, he naturally should be identified with a title. With many others, it is pride, an attitude of haughtiness that they are to be called by a title because of who they *think they are*; however, if we take a good look at the attitude of the leadership within the scriptures concerning this matter, you will see a vast difference in attitude.

In writing to the Church concerning the Revelation of Jesus Christ, John, the apostle, makes this statement:

*" I John, who am also your **brother**, and companion in tribulation, and in the Kingdom and patience of Jesus Christ, was in the isle that is called Patmos, for the Word of God, and the testimony of Jesus Christ"* (Rev 1:9).

John did not identify himself as Apostle John or by some great, long, drawn-out title such as Reverend-Doctor-Preacher-Bishop John. He identified himself as a **BROTHER**. This is unlike the renowned preachers of today who MUST have a title in front of their name, when none of the major leaders in scripture identified themselves as Apostle, Prophet, or Pastor so-and so; *a title never preceded their name.*

Paul never addresses himself as Apostle Paul. When he wrote to the churches, he always addressed the letters as Paul, an apostle..." or "Paul, called to be an apostle..." (1 Cor. 1:1; 2 Cor.1: 1; Gal. 1:1; Eph..1: 1;Col., 1:1; 1 Tim., 1:1; 2 Tim. 1:1;).

Even better, there were times when he addressed himself as "Paul, a **SERVANT** of God...." (Rom..1: 1; Philli.1: 1; Tit. 1:1).

The same went for James: "James, a **SERVANT** of God and of the Lord Jesus Christ..." (Jas. 1:1); and Peter: "Simon Peter, a **SERVANT** and apostle of Jesus Christ..." (2 Pet. 1:1).in 1 Peter 5:1, in addressing the eldership, Peter also says, *"The elders which are among you, I exhort,* **who am also an elder***, and a witness of the sufferings of Christ..."* (KJV).

He did not identify himself as Apostle Peter in his writings to try to enforce his apostleship or to prove who he was. He did not even identify himself as a chief elder. He identified himself as **ONE OF THE ELDERS**, not as someone who was above everyone else.

This attitude in our spiritual forefathers is greatly different from those in leadership today.

In no way am I saying that we should never address the gifts and callings that God has placed in our lives to accomplish His Will. It is good for a leader to know the various gifts and graces that God has deposited in him. 2 Peter 1:10 says, *"Wherefore the rather, brethren, give diligence to make your* **calling** *and election sure...."* (KJV)

Paul also stated: *"Whereunto I am ordained a* **preacher***, and an* **apostle***, (I speak the truth in Christ and lie not;) a* **teacher** *of the Gentiles in faith and verity"* (1Tim.2: 7 KJV).

Paul knew what his particular anointing was. He knew what his work was in the Lord to do. Not once did he state himself as Apostle Paul in any of his letters, but he was "Paul, an apostle…his name is Paul and he does the work of an apostle.

No one's first name is Apostle or Evangelist so-and-so, yet many continue to stick these titles in front of their name for identification. Apostle, Prophet, Pastor is not your name or who you are, **IT'S WHAT YOU DO! Yet many believe that this is who they are.**

This is not good, especially if, for one reason or another, the Lord shuts down a man's ministry for a season. I have known men of God whose, after years of ministering, for one reason or another, their work that they were involved in gets shut down, or they may have been asked to sit down for a season. When this happened, they may have had to find themselves a job for a little while until God re-instated them back into the work. But during this time of trial, some became disoriented and seemed lost as to what to do with themselves, simply because all they knew how to do for years and years was minister. With that gone, they did not know what to do with themselves. Their identification was in what they were anointed to do, but not in who they really were.

Our identification should be in Jesus Christ and the fact that we are sons and daughters of our Heavenly Father…not in a five-fold ministry gift! We should never identify only with a five-fold ministry gift!

There are fellowships I know of that have gone way overboard with titles. There is one such, and I will not name names, where many of the believers who fellowship there call the man of God there The Great Apostle.

Although I strongly believe in apostolic ministry today, no man should take this honor unto himself. Hebrews 3:1 says this, "*Wherefore holy brethren, partakers of the heavenly calling, consider **THE APOSTLE** and **HIGH PRIEST** of our profession, **JESUS CHRIST**"*. Jesus and Jesus alone is the only one that should ever be called **THE GREAT APOSTLE. Yet even He does not require us to call Him by a title. We call Him by His first name...JESUS!**

The Word Reverend

Church leaders today are caught up in a titles-mania to where it's almost considered a sin to call them by their real names.

Of all the titles known to the world and church leaders, reverend is the most popular, just as it has been for hundreds and hundreds of years. The word reverend precedes the name of the majority of spiritual leaders around the world, be they Pentecostal, Charismatic, Baptist, Evangelical or Catholic. Yet the best reference to the word reverend in the Bible is in Psalm.111: 9 and this referred to the Lord God Almighty and Him alone: "*He sent redemption unto his people: he has commanded His covenant forever: holy and **REVEREND** is His name*".

No man of God, throughout any of the scriptures, ever stuck the title Reverend on the front of their name.

Britannica-Webster Dictionary defines reverend as "worthy of reverence"; reverence means respect felt or shown, or a feeling of worshipful respect. Strong's Exhaustive Concordance of the Bible has the Hebrew word *yare* (pronounced yaw-ray, number 3372 and 3373 in the Hebrew and Chaldee dictionary), which *means to fear, revere, frighten; to be had in reverence; put in fear or afraid.* So what a leader is basically saying when he tags reverend in front of his name is that his name should be feared, reverenced, and that the people around him should have the "most worshipful respect" towards him. **Brethren, this ought to not be.** The only one that should have this kind of title *is the Lord God Himself and Jesus Christ, for His name is higher than any other*!

"Wherefore God also hath highly exalted Him and given Him a name that is above every name. That at the name of Jesus, every knee should bow, of things in heaven, and things in earth, and things under the earth. And that every tongue should confess that Jesus Christ is Lord to the glory of God the Father" (Phil. 2: 9-11).

Let this not be misunderstood. I am in no way saying that leaders and those who have been given authority to rule should not be honored and respected. The scripture says, *"Let the elders that rule well be counted worthy of **double honour**, especially they who labour in the Word and doctrine..."* (1 Tim. 5:17 KJV).

This scripture also connotes making sure that those in leadership have adequate financial support (see 5092 in Strong's Exhaustive Concordance). So let it never be thought that there is something wrong in supporting those in leadership with our prayers AND OUR FINANCES, *if* God has instructed you to do so. The problem begins when the boundary line is crossed; when we move out of the realm of honoring those leaders, and move over into the realm of idolatry. Honoring a leader does not mean we have to constantly address him by a title.

Having to constantly address spiritual leaders by a title only makes it seem like they are untouchable, and many believe that this is the way it should be.

Over the years, I have heard some say that they believe there should be a big gap between the leadership and the sheep. Having put this concept into practice, it made leaders appear unapproachable. The result of this has been a people who are intimidated by those in leadership, and you can see it in them.

I have seen and talked to Christians so intimidated by their leaders, that when face-to-face with them, they could barely talk, stumbling over their words. Or as some say, when they see a leader coming towards them, they get nervous jitters, and butterflies in their stomach, and it's not because they have some secret sin in their lives and they cannot look them in the eye because of it, but it's an inordinate fear based out of an idolatrous heart.

This needs to be overcome on the part of the people of God, and as for those in leadership, ask yourself this: why do you need to be distinguished with a title? Is it scriptural to insist that everyone in leadership be addressed by titles? What is your motive behind acquiring the title of Doctor? Is it right for you to stick Reverend in front of your name just because preachers have been associated with the word for hundreds of years? Just because the terminology has been around for a long time, does that make it right by Scripture?

Authority Recognized by the Spirit

Recognition of one's authority is not known by titles. Recognition of authority is perceived in the Spirit. These things are not known outwardly, for there are many that have a title of a leader, but not the call. It also has nothing to do with what a man of God wears.

Collars around the neck, long robes, the wearing of crowns or a dark suite with a fancy tie does not prove a man's authority as a leader. Carrying around a shepherd's staff does not qualify you to have the authority of a shepherd.

Wearing the same clothes as a certain man of God will not give you the same authority as that man of God .To show you how the spirit of idolatry can carry over even into this realm of clothes or garments, let me tell you a story…

Imitating the Anointing

I was first born-again and Spirit-filled under a powerful ministry many years ago. The man of God who was its leader at the time had a very flamboyant personality. He loved to wear expensive suites, ties, jewelry, and fancy white shoes. He was a dynamic, anointed preacher that moved in the gifts of Healing and Word of Knowledge in a most powerful way. Some of the most powerful healing-miracles that I have ever witnessed first-hand, I saw during that time in my life under that ministry.

The pastor had a certain walk, a certain way of talking and he spoke many clichés. When you were around him, you could sense a mighty presence of God upon him, possibly because he often went away for thirty day fasts before the Lord. The sad thing about this; however, was that, despite the great things that were going on there, there was not much spiritual fathering going on in those days, and many of us went around with areas in our lives that were never dealt with or touched: areas of rebellion, sin and idolatry to name a few.

So when many of the young men went out from that local church to start their own ministries, many of them attempted to imitate the man of God from whom they came under. They tried to wear the same clothes he wore, walk like he walked, talk like he talked, and use the same clichés. Some even tried to wear the same white shoes that he wore, hoping, that by mimicking that man of God, they would reproduce the same results as he did. Needless to say, many failed miserably in their ministries and many who started out strong in the Lord had their faith shipwrecked.

You cannot reproduce the results of what God is dong in another man's life just by wearing the same clothes he wears, or talking his talk. This is an aspect of the spirit of idolatry, **when we try to be like someone else instead of who God created us to be**.

Unfortunately, a lack of Biblical spiritual fathering in those days caused many of the young men of that day who had a genuine five-fold call of God on their lives to have identity problems.

They never quite allowed Jesus Christ to develop their **own individuality** and bring them into their own spiritual inheritance. Instead, they became clones of that man's ministry and his personality.

Ironically, some of this still goes on today. Many still go out having never allowed Jesus Christ to develop their own individuality.

They look like clones of those whose ministry they are under. This is not being likeminded, like we are commanded to be with each other as the Scriptures teaches us Philippians 2:2 says, **"Fulfill ye my joy, that ye be likeminded, having the same love, being of one accord, of one mind."**

Hear, O men of God, all you who are being raised up as spiritual leaders today: **YOU BECOME LIKEMINDED BY FATHERING OR SPITITUAL MENTORING; NOT BY BECOMING A CLONE OF ANOTHER MAN'S PERSONALITY AND MINISTRY!**

Paul the apostle was also a spiritual father (1 Cor.4: 15 -17). Look at what he has to say about Timothy, who was one of his sons in the faith:

*"But I trust the Lord Jesus to send Timotheus shortly unto you, that I also may be of good comfort, when I know your state. **For I have no man likeminded**, who will naturally care for your state. For all seek their own, not the things which are Jesus Christ's. But ye know the proof of him, **that, as a son with the father**, he hath served with me in the gospel"* (Phil. 2:19-22 KJV).

Let us consider and pray about all these things, as we move on and learn how to be delivered from idolatry.

7
OVERCOMING IDOLATRY

With all that's been said, how do we conquer idolatry of this type? Here are answers to help us overcome this problem.

Steps Towards Deliverance

Number One: **You must have a solid walk with God.** Not just a superficial churchgoing conviction, but a heartfelt passion for Jesus Christ and a solid relationship with Him to where you KNOW Him, not just by doctrine or as a historical entity that you have a belief system in. The devils believe that as well (Jas. 2:19); but a relationship that has been developed so that you know the gentle voice of His Spirit in your own heart. Many do not realize that God is a person and He desires our fellowship and praise. The primary reason man was created upon the Earth was to fellowship with his Creator. It is His desire that we get to know Him.

"And **they shall teach no more every man his neighbor, and every man his brother, saying know the Lord, for they shall all know Me, from the least of them unto the greatest of them saith the Lord**..." (Jer. 31:34 KJV)

"And **I will give them an heart to know Me, that I am the Lord. And they shall be My people and I will be their God…**" (Jer. 24:7 KJV)

Number Two: **You must have a strong and solid foundation in the Word of God.** All things that you hear, any doctrine, dogma, or supposed new thing that comes to you *must be filtered by the Scriptures!* ***The Scriptures are the final authority on any matter.*** It does not matter what voices you may be hearing, if it does not line up with the Word of God, **then you do not have to subject yourself to it.**

"**Beloved, believe not every spirit, but try the spirits whether they are of God: because many false prophets are gone out into the world…**" (1 John 4:1 KJV).

No matter how sincere anything may be, or how beautiful a certain doctrine or revelation may sound, *it must be proven to be scripturally sound.* The Bible speaks that much false doctrine will go out in the last days to deceive many.

"**Now the Spirit speaketh expressly, that in the latter times, many shall depart from the faith, giving heed to seducing spirits and doctrines of devils…**" (1 Tim. 4:1 KJV)

Many are swayed about, misled and confused very easily because they do not know the Word. Look at how Jesus responded to the devils temptations while he was in the wilderness:

"**Then** *was Jesus led up of the spirit into the wilderness to be tempted of the devil. And when he had fasted forty days and forty nights, he was afterward an hungred. And when the tempter came to him, he said, if thou be the Son of God, command that these stones be* *turned to bread. But he answered and said,* **It is written**, *Man shall not live by bread alone, but by every word that proceedeth out of the mouth of God. Then the devil taketh him up into the holy city, and setteth him on a pinnacle of the temple, and saith unto him, If thou be the Son of God, cast thyself down:* **for it is written**, *He shall give his angels charge concerning thee: and in their hands they shall bear thee up, lest at any time though dash thy foot against a stone. Jesus said unto him,* **It is written again**, *Thou shalt not tempt the Lord thy God. Again, the devil taketh him up into an exceeding high mountain, and sheweth him all the kingdoms of the world, and the glory of them; And saith unto him, All these things will I give thee, if thou wilt fall down and worship me. Then saith Jesus unto him, Get thee hence, Satan:* **for it is written**, *Thou shalt worship the Lord thy God, and him only shalt thou serve. Then the devil leaveth him, and, behold, angels came and ministered unto him."* (Matt. 4:1-11 KJV)

Notice, with each temptation that came, Jesus responded with "**it is written**..." *This should be how every Christian responds to deception and false doctrine when it comes their way.* Jesus knew the Holy Scriptures; therefore he could not be swayed by Satan's trickery and twisting of the Scriptures.

There is one irrefutable way of knowing whether what you are hearing is from God or not, and that is by knowing the following: "*For there are three that bear record in Heaven, the Father, the Word and the Holy Ghost.* **And these three are one**" (1 John 5:7 KJV).

Our Heavenly Father will **never** *contradict His own Word or the Holy Ghost.* They are ONE! Knowing this will greatly help you. We must also realize that ALL Scripture (not some) is given by inspiration of God. 2 Timothy 3:16-17 says,: *"All Scripture is given by **inspiration** of God and is profitable for doctrine, reproof, for correction, for instruction in righteousness, that the man of God may be perfect, thoroughly furnished unto all good works."* The word inspiration here means "God breathed", and as the Amplified Bible states in verse 16, the scripture can be used for **"correction of error"**. You can always check for error in anything you hear by the Scriptures. God's Word will never change! It is eternally set.

"My covenant will I not break, nor alter the thing that has gone out of my lips" (Ps.89:34 KJV)

"Heaven and earth shall pass away, but my words shall not pass away" (Matt.24:35 KJV)

"…if he called them gods, unto whom the Word of God came, and **the Scriptures cannot be broken**…" (John 10:35 KJV)

Know Yourself

Number Three: You must know who you are. **You must know that your identification is with Jesus Christ,** not some spiritual movement, a strong, charismatic leader or your natural heritage. You may actually be a part of all of these to some degree, but these are not truly who you as an individual. You are a child of the Most High God, a son or daughter by adoption because of what Jesus Christ did for us on the cross (see Gal. 4:5-6; Eph. 1:5). And you must realize that God is looking to bring the consummation of all things in Heaven and Earth **"IN HIM"**…Jesus Christ! (Eph. 1:10 -12). Our identity is **in Him!**

Healthy Understanding of God's Authority

Number Four: **You must have a healthy understanding of authority**. Lest anyone misunderstand this book and believe that it is teaching rebellion to those in authority, let some things be clarified. In no way, form or fashion is this book coming forth to teach rebelliousness toward those in civil or spiritual authority. I am a strong believer in **everyone** being **responsible to** someone in authority, lest you become a lone wolf. The Scriptures make it very clear:

*"Let **EVERY SOUL** be **SUBJECT** to the higher powers. For there is no power but of God. For whosoever resisteth the ordinance of God; And they that resist shall receive to themselves damnation. **For rulers are not a terror to good works, but to evil.** Wilt thou then not be afraid of the power? Do that which is good and thou shalt have praise of the same. For he is a minister of God to thee for good..."* (Rom. 13:1-4 KJV).

*"Obey **them that have the rule over you, and submit yourselves**: For they watch for your souls as they that must give an account, that they may do it with joy and not with grief; for it is unprofitable for you"* (Heb. 13:17 KJV).

So there is subjection to authority, **but what we must learn is to subject ourselves to their authority, not their control.** Idolatry often comes in the heart of a people, because some have a twisted concept of authority. They may have grown up in a household where their parents were extremely abusive and controlling, where it was a dictatorship instead of a stable, loving home. So in their minds, anyone in authority represents what they may have grown up to know, and consequently, they may fall for a leader that manifests this type of behavior under the deception that he is representing God.

Subjecting to True Spiritual Authority, not Control

Number Five: **Surround and submit yourself to Godly counselors.** As stated in an earlier chapter, there is safety in a multitude of counselors (Prov. 11:14). It is always good to be in relationship with those who truly love and care about you. Leaders need to surround themselves with people who care about you, whether they are part of their eldership, staff or just plain friends who love them. Regardless, they must be people that love them enough to confront them when there are real issues in their lives; they cannot be a bunch of "yes men".

"Yes men" or women will always justify unhealthy behavioral patterns either through their own selfishness, a lack of judgment or by letting friendship blind them to the truth. Personal accountability without control can be a beautiful way to keep checks and balances in our lives, especially when there is a leader who may have some serious problems with control.

Recovering from Becoming an Idol

Now concerning leadership and their role in idolatry, how does a spiritual leader deal with the issue of idolatry when faced with it? One example is to look at the lifestyle of Jesus Christ and see how He responded to certain situations. After performing the great miracle of reproducing the loaves amongst a great multitude, (John 6:1-13) look at how He reacted to the people. *"Then those men, when they had seen the miracle that Jesus did, said, this is of a truth that prophet that should come into the world. When Jesus therefore perceived that they would come and take Him by force, to make Him a king,* **He departed again into a mountain himself alone**" (John 6:14-15). The Amplified Bible says He "**withdrew**" Himself. Now here is the King of kings and Lord of lords withdrawing himself when He knew the people were coming to make Him a king. He had every right to be a king because He is The King of kings, but he knew that they would force Him into something pre-mature, **so He withdrew Himself.**

Any leader that perceives idolatry in the heart of a people or a person should utilize this principle. If idolatry is in the heart of a people toward a leader, it might be wisdom for that man of God to withdraw himself for a season. He may not necessarily have to step down from the ministry, but temporarily obscure himself

Why: to wean the people of God from being in idolatry to their leader. Some do need to be weaned in this area.

Some time ago at a particular local church that I belonged to, the senior pastor went away for a couple of weeks. Although several of the elders of the Church, along with a trusted visiting minister, maintained the church business and brought forth the Word, all I heard from some of the members during that time was "when is the pastor coming back...I miss my pastor...I cannot listen to anyone, but the pastor... the word is not as good as the pastor's..."

Although the Word brought forth by the visiting minister and the elders of the Church was dynamic and timely, many of the people complained all the way up until the senior pastor returned.

This is not good. The people of God should learn to love and receive *the Word of God* **regardless of who it comes from,** as long as it is sound doctrine and it is a word in due season. This was a case of a people who have a problem with idolatry. Some were completely shut down or would not come to church simply because the pastor was not there.

There is no problem with people loving and missing their leaders when they go away. That's natural. *Naturally*, you will grow fond of those that are over you in the Lord. I am in no way saying all feelings of fondness for leadership are bad. It becomes a problem if the people of God *will not listen to any other minister and refuse to come to fellowship just because the senior pastor is not there.* It is a problem when there are constant criticisms and comparisons to other leaders and men of God, when you believe **your** pastor is better than any other man of God. I have actually seen where the people would not pay their tithes when the senior pastor was out of town. I actually recall one of the deacons having to call up the pastor of the church just so he would give the people an okay to pay their tithes and give in the offering because as long as he was gone, **THEY REFUSED TO DO IT!**

We ought to pay our tithes and give in offerings regardless, **for we give unto God, NOT MAN.** This is a great test of our hearts, to see just what motivates us, or why we do what we do. Do we fellowship where we do because we believe that God joined us there or are we there because we are caught up in the charisma of a leader's call or personality? Did Jesus Christ set you there in that particular work of God (1 Cor. 12:18), or are you there for other self-centered reasons?

These are questions we must ponder and if we find that our motives are not correct in this area, let us repent before our Heavenly Father, ask Him to clean up our motives and set us in the place where He has called us to be. We must ask Him to wean us from all idolatry and give us a right spirit toward those in leadership.

How does a leader recover himself from idolatry, if he comes to the realization that he is manifesting a controlling spirit rather than the authority of God? The first step is that **he must repent of this behavior and sincerely ask God to cleanse his heart**. If he cannot do this alone, it would be advisable to seek out godly counsel and prayer, particularly from those whom God has joined him to, those that he may trust, to help him through this process of humbling himself. Regardless, **that leader absolutely must humble himself when it comes to this area, no matter what it takes. It does not matter how flamboyant, strong or charismatic one's personality is. Personality is still subject to the principles in the Word.**

"Humble yourselves in the sight of the Lord, and He shall lift you up." (James 4:10 KJV)

Even if it means stepping out of the arena of ministry for a season, do whatever it takes to get this area dealt with. Don't let pride hinder you from this for *"[p]ride goeth before destruction and a haughty spirit before a fall"* (Prov.16:18 KJV).

"...God resisteth the proud, but giveth grace to the humble..." (Jas. 4:6b KJV)

If a leader refuses to humble himself and be corrected in this area, even if he has been confronted on this matter and rebelliously believes that he is right, then a principle will go into effect as stated in Matthew 21:42-44:

"Jesus saith unto them, did ye never read the scriptures, the Stone which the builders rejected, the same is become the Head of the corner: this is the Lords doing and it is marvelous in our eyes? Therefore say I unto you, the kingdom of God will be taken from you and given to a nation bringing forth the fruits thereof. **And whosoever shall fall on this Stone, shall be broken: but on whomsoever it shall fall, it will grind him to powder.**" (KJV)

Now we know that Jesus Christ is Chief Cornerstone; the Stone that was rejected of men. (Eph. 2:20; 1 Pet. 2:4-6). If a man falls upon this Stone, then he shall be broken (humbled), for *"…the sacrifices of God are a broken spirit: a broken and contrite heart, O God thou shalt not despise"* (Ps. 51:17 KJV) and *"The Lord is close to those that are of a broken heart and saves such as are crushed with sorrow for sin and are humbly and thoroughly penitent"* (Ps. 34:18 AMP). A great work will take place in his heart and he'll come into new levels of enjoying Jesus Christ and His people; but if he resists God in this area and will not bow his spirit down in this area, then the Stone will fall upon him and "grind him to powder". The Amplified Bible says *"… but he on whom it falls will be crushed to powder [and it will winnow him, scattering him like the dust]"*.

Seeking honor from God

Hear O men of God that have problems with lordship and control. You either **HUMBLE YOURSELF OR BE HUMBLED**. If you humble yourself, you will have a good turnaround and a renewed spirit made right; but if you refuse, you will go on believing you are something you are not, and will take a place in the people of God's heart that was never given to you by the Lord. You will go on deceiving and being deceived, but the *day will come* when God *will remove your kingdom from you and shake your world.*

We are living in days when **God will not be mocked** no matter what area it is in, but there one thing that *He will not have*, and that is anyone **taking His place as Lord in His people's lives**. The day will come when, in order to preserve you, He will expose you for what you really are, even if it means shutting down the ministry that you so love. We have already seen some of Gods men humbled, or crushed to powder on national T.V. They would not humble themselves, so God humbled them.

And please do not say this is not the love of God. It is the extreme love of God. *For God in His love for his leaders would rather have them publicly exposed and humiliated and have him **get delivered**,* then to allow him to go on in their deception.

We must be ever so careful as to not cross the line between honor and idolatry. The scriptures *do* tell us to "honor all men" (1 Pet. 2:17). We are to also honor those elders that rule the house of God well (1 Tim. 5:17), but never are we to allow that respect to turn into idolatry, and never are we to submit to their control.

O Church of the Living God let us learn to seek the honor that comes from God only. If we do, we'll be blessed in all things.

Amen!

"How can ye believe, which receive honour one from another and seek not the honour that cometh from God only?" (John 5:44 KJV)

"Little children, keep yourselves from idols. Amen." (1 John 5:21 KJV)

www.ingramcontent.com/pod-product-compliance
Ingram Content Group UK Ltd.
Pitfield, Milton Keynes, MK11 3LW, UK
UKHW022232230426
I2048UKWH000178A/1217